The Story of the Dragonfly

Story by Debbie Sorrells
Illustrations by Laura Sorrells

Illustrations by Laura Sorrells

First Edition

Hardcover ISBN: 978-1-62720-455-2
Paperback ISBN: 978-1-62720-456-9

Published by Apprentice House Press

Loyola University Maryland
4501 N. Charles Street, Baltimore, MD 21210
410.617.5265
www.ApprenticeHouse.com
info@ApprenticeHouse.com

Dedicated to Our True Heroes
Police, Firefighters, EMTs, Teachers & Invested Parents

In Memory of Officer Amy Sorrells Caprio
EOW 5/21/2018

Foreword

Major Deanna L. Chemelli
Baltimore County Police Department

As a little girl, Officer Amy Sorrells Caprio was very active and loved playing sports. She began playing soccer when she was in the 1st grade and quickly acclimated to being a goalie. Even at a young age, Amy showed that she wanted to be a "protector," even if it was only an 8 foot by 24 foot soccer goal. The goalie for her soccer team at Loch Raven High School, a framed goalie jersey is now displayed in the hallway leading to the gymnasium. Her number, 24, is now retired.

Amy attended Towson University and graduated in 2010 with a degree in Exercise Science. Shortly after graduation, Amy began working at St. Joseph's Hospital, in Towson, Maryland.

As much as Amy loved being an Out-Patient Rehabilitation Technician, she still yearned for something more. Like a goalie blocking a penalty kick and protecting the goal, Amy wanted to have the same impact on her community, to protect it. In 2014, Amy joined the Baltimore County Police Department to pursue her dream of being a police officer. After graduating from the police academy, Amy was assigned to the Essex Precinct, where she worked for 2 years. In the hopes of increasing her knowledge of the communities within Baltimore County, Amy transferred to the Parkville Precinct in 2017. As a young officer, Amy quickly proved herself to be a very capable police officer and earned the respect and admiration of her fellow officers and supervisors.

When not handling a call for service or investigating a crime, Amy could often be found spending time with the children at a local elementary school. Amy would read books with the children, play with them at recess, or assist them in the cafeteria during lunch time. Amy

Hero (heer-oh) — noun.

A person admired for achievements and noble qualities; one who shows great courage.

was described as a loyal, kind, hard-working, inspiring, dedicated, selfless, and community-oriented police officer.

On May 21, 2018, Officer Amy Caprio responded to a call for a suspicious vehicle in Perry Hall, Maryland. A second call to 9-1-1 confirmed that a home was being burglarized by four suspects associated with a vehicle, which was later determined to be a stolen Jeep Wrangler. Officer Caprio arrived in the area and located the suspect vehicle. She then followed the vehicle into a cul-de-sac, where the suspect turned his vehicle facing Officer Caprio's patrol vehicle. She exited her vehicle, with her weapon drawn, and ordered the suspect out of the vehicle. The suspect opened the driver's door of the Jeep Wrangler, as though he was complying with Officer Caprio's orders. When Officer Caprio approached the suspect, he immediately retreated into the Jeep Wrangler and accelerated towards her. The suspect driver ducked down behind the dashboard and continued accelerating towards Officer Caprio, fatally striking her.

Officer Caprio, age 29, was killed in the line-of-duty, while serving the citizens of Baltimore County, Maryland. Officer Caprio died doing a job that she truly loved. Police work was her calling, it was her passion, and it was her dream. She will always be remembered as a loving daughter, wife, friend, and fellow officer. Family and friends of Amy would encourage us all to emulate her traits and simply…"Be Amy."

Officer Amy Sorrells Caprio #5785, of the Baltimore County Police Department, believed in serving and protecting others, and for that, she sacrificed everything.

September 2022

Once upon a time, there was a little girl who grew up with two sisters, dogs, and cats.

The little girl loved school, making friends, and playing soccer.

As the little girl grew, she kept playing soccer, enjoyed hiking through the woods, and making more friends.

One day, the girl was old enough to drive a jeep, work at an animal hospital, read lots of books (especially Harry Potter), and go to college.

After college, this young lady worked in a hospital helping people get stronger with exercise. She would bike ride, kayak, and spend time with her friends.

One day, she told her family that she was going to be a police woman.

She worked very hard at the police school/academy. Some days she came home smiling and happy, but always sore, sweaty, and very tired.

TU
Hospital
POLICE

She made many friends, and friends help each other, care about each other, and make each other better people.

The evening Officer Amy graduated from the Baltimore County Police Academy was a very happy time for everyone because her dream to become a police woman had finally come true.

She was finally the person she wanted to be - someone to help other people and animals, to protect them, keep them safe, and be their friend.

Officer Amy loved her job as a police woman, even though it was sometimes very hard and very dangerous work.

She made many friends with other police, children, and people in the community.

One day, some bad guys stole a car and went to different houses, stealing things that did not belong to them.

Officer Amy went to answer the call for help because she wanted to stop the bad guys and protect the good people who lived there.

Officer Amy was able to stop the bad guys; she gave her life trying to catch them. Her police family worked very hard together to find and arrest them.

The day Officer Amy was buried, a large dragonfly flew past her friends, around the car that was carrying her, and then flew over to where her blue family of police were standing. It seemed like the dragonfly was checking on Officer Amy's families and friends.

Caprio

After that day, a dragonfly visited the house of someone who was with Officer Amy when she was hit by the car. It would sit on the porch railing or chair, as if to say, “I’m still here.”

A dragonfly would sometimes visit Dunkin' Donuts when officers met to have coffee and share good memories.

Hiking in the woods, a dragonfly was watching over an officer, and one was found sitting on a kayak, and one on a boat with others.

coffee

Dragonflies were present at a friend's wedding.

They were seen swarming around a special person's car at the beach. Dragonflies would often visit Officer Amy's nephews while they played in their pool.

A dragonfly even visited the playground being dedicated to Amy while it was being built.

It was as if “someone” was supervising the job to make sure everything was safe and perfect for you.

Gunpowder
Elementary

Dragonflies have visited many people.

If you keep your eyes open, you will see dragonflies, too. They will make you smile, give you hope, and remind you that Officer Amy is still here with you.

Dragonflies are messengers that symbolize love, strength, and hope. They promise to watch over people.

There is a legend that tells us that dragonflies were given an extra set of wings so that angels could ride on their backs.

So when you see a dragonfly, think of it as a reminder that an angel from heaven is visiting you and keeping you safe.

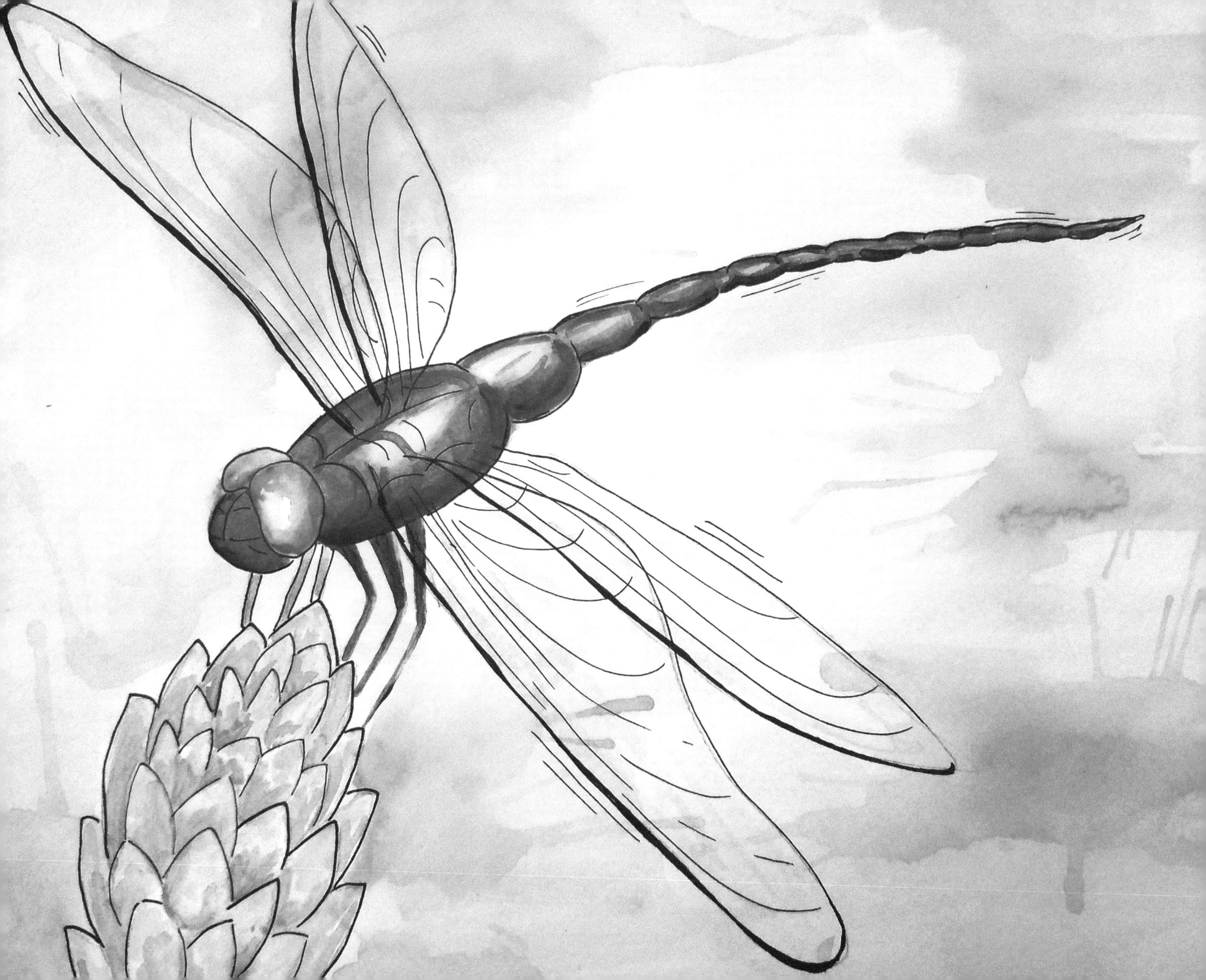

Amy Sorrells Caprio

5/27/1988 - 5/21/2018

About the Sorrells Family

written by a close family friend

Families don't get much more salt of the earth than the Sorrells. Married in 1981, Debbie and her husband Garry have been fixtures of the Baltimore County community for their entire lives. Garry was a general contractor as well as an Eagle Scout with the Boy Scouts of America, while Debbie earned her degree as a registered nurse specializing in special needs children.

Soon, Kristin came along, followed by Laura and Amy, two years apart. All very different yet all amazingly caring and inquisitive ladies, they each carved their own paths in life. All three ladies received degrees and graduated from Towson University. Kristin, in Speech Pathology; Laura, in Art Education; Amy, in Exercise Science.

Amy soon pursued her dream of becoming a police officer, and in 2014, she achieved that dream. Only four short years later, Amy was tragically killed while responding to a burglary call on May 21, 2018. The suspect intentionally struck her in an attempt to flee the scene. During her career with Baltimore County, she worked out of Precincts 11 (Essex) and 8 (Parkville). Ofc. Caprio was awarded Officer of the Month twice, having been nominated three times. She was the first female officer killed in the line of duty in the history of the department, and was awarded the Medal Of Honor posthumously for her heroism and sacrifice. She left behind her family as well as her husband, Tim.

As time moved on, Debbie was compelled to write this book. Amy and her family love dragonflies. Once the words were roughed out, Laura took over and illustrated the book. This is a labor of love.

This book is written in, and dedicated to, Amy's memory.

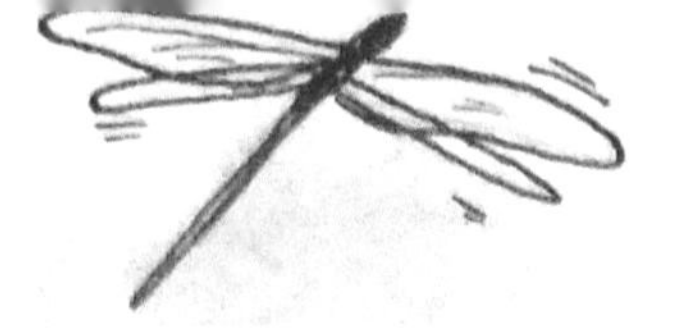

What's your dragonfly story?

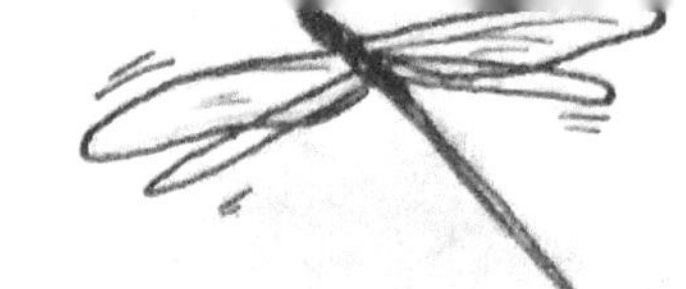

Apprentice House is the country's only campus-based, student-staffed book publishing company. Directed by professors and industry professionals, it is a nonprofit activity of the Communication Department at Loyola University Maryland.

Using state-of-the-art technology and an experiential learning model of education, Apprentice House publishes books in untraditional ways.This dual responsibility as publishers and educators creates an unprecedented collaborative environment among faculty and students, while teaching tomorrow's editors, designers, and marketers.

Eclectic and provocative, Apprentice House titles intend to entertain as well as spark dialogue on a variety of topics. Financial contributions to sustain the press's work are welcomed.Contributions are tax deductible to the fullest extent allowed by the IRS.

To learn more about Apprentice House books or to obtain submission guidelines, please visit www.apprenticehouse.com.

Apprentice House
Communication Department
Loyola University Maryland
4501 N. Charles Street
Baltimore, MD 21210
410-617-5265
info@apprenticehouse.com
www.apprenticehouse.com

CPSIA information can be obtained
at www.ICGtesting.com
Printed in the USA
BVHW062315151122
651776BV00001B/1

9781627204552